ULTIMATE PARENTS GUIDE TO
TRAINING
for
LACROSSE

BY

SEAN KELLY

CONTENTS

INTRODUCTION

Lacrosse continues to increase in popularity, but the amount of training programs that work do not. Being one of the fastest growing sports in today's society, there should be some type of program available to parents who want to help their child improve their physical skills as well as develop a high lacrosse IQ.

The lacrosse players who want to commit to a lacrosse specific strength training program and lacrosse specific skills program that is equally committed to them should read this book; I know what you need to do, and how you need to do it. However, the bottom line is that your child will need to do it. If they choose to, the sky is truly the limit on how far they can go in the game of Lacrosse.

There are various lacrosse training programs and books available, but most of those documents or programs lack what a player really needs: the coaching or instruction necessary to be great. Lacrosse is more than a sport; it is more than a game. Knowing how to run the field, or how to beat your man is only part of the training; the mental aspect of Lacrosse is just as important as the skills that are necessary to play the game, if not more. Without possessing a high Lacrosse IQ to go along with your high level of skill, you will not reach your true potential.

With years of experience in this field,

my training program at Sean Kelly's Performance Center has been helping countless lacrosse players realize their potential in the sport by focusing on their mental approach to the game, as well as the physical aspect of the sport, and their athletic success. Parents continuously choose my skills training program and read my book because this program has helped countless players reach their full potential by drastically improving their physical skills, while providing them with the necessary knowledge of the game.

Lacrosse is more than a game; lacrosse is a sport that energizes the player on the inside, as well as the outside. Lacrosse is a sport that helps build mental strength as well as physical power. Lacrosse is a sport that many individuals play, but most of those individuals do not truly understand the sport itself.

Throughout this book, you will learn the following:

- skills training
- goal setting
- sport specifics
- nutritional dos and don'ts
- the mental toughness guidelines that every lacrosse player and athlete should possess.

If you are ready to take your game to that next level, this book will help you do just that, as long as you are fully committed to the game, as well as the training process. Do not worry about wasting time on another program that does not work, because our program will help you get to that next level by focusing on improving your overall mental toughness.

Finally, there is a coach here for you; a program that will help your child learn what it truly means to practice and make a commitment; and finally, a program that GUARANTEES solutions to the problems!

CHAPTER ONE: SKILLS TRAINING

Do you have the skills that are necessary for a lacrosse player to perform at a high level game in and game out? If the answer is yes, then I'm sure that you have worked very hard to get to that level. However, if you do not possess these skills and you want to, then you will need to know exactly what you need to practice in order to obtain them.

Remember that practice does not make perfect; practice makes habits.

So if you want to be great, and you

have the willingness to learn, then this lacrosse program is exactly what you need. Improvement begins with you, and only you. If you want to stay ahead of your competition, you will need to practice. If you want to achieve a certain goal in the sport of Lacrosse, identify what that goal is and begin taking the necessary steps to achieve it. Many youth and High School level lacrosse players currently play games 80% of the time, but they only spend 20% of the time practicing. This will almost always guarantee that the players will not improve. If you are not practicing on improving your weaknesses and bad habits in between games, then how are you going to see any improvement? Knowledge is power; this statement is true on many levels, including the lacrosse sport level. The techniques and proficiencies that each lacrosse player should possess are exactly what this portion of the book will teach you. Remember that repetition is the mother of skill. If you have bad habits, it is time to replace them with good habits. Some examples of bad habits are bringing your stick behind your head, cradling with your bottom hand, and shooting side arm. Failing to correct these bad habits and constantly learning new skills could be something that limits your growth as a lacrosse player. It is important not to limit yourself, because doing so could impact your effectiveness in the game, as well as your ability to advance as a lacrosse player.

I cannot stress the importance of mastering the fundamentals. If you never stop practicing the basics, then you won't have to go back to them. The skills we will be helping you master at SKPC include:

- Catching
- Passing
- Cradling
- Defending
- Shooting
- Dodging
- Goalie Skills
- Speed Training
- Scooping
- Lacrosse IQ (understanding the rules of the game, basic concepts and what you should be doing in different situations)
- and more…

There are many claims made by lacrosse coaches, and players; do not believe all of those claims because some are actually myths. Some of the top myths associated with lacrosse include:

- The best way to score is shooting at the top corner. FALSE. Although picking corners looks great, it is not always the best shot to take. Good goalies need to be challenged. Overhand bounce shots keep the goalies guessing and make him move his feet.

- I don't need to be equally as strong with both hands. FALSE. Even with the success that many Native American and Canadian players have had while exclusively using their dominant hand, we are not all as talented as Lyle Thompson. Having an equal amount of comfort performing all of the basic skills of the game with both your right and left hands is still needed.

- Lacrosse players don't need to lift weights. FALSE. I would like to think that nobody actually believes this anymore, but getting as big, strong and fast as possible still does not seem like a number 1 priority in the culture of younger lacrosse players. Huge mistake. Take a look at the physique of Paul Rabil and the workout regimen he follows and then tell me that lifting weights doesn't help you improve at the game of lacrosse.

- Division I is where all the best lacrosse players play in college and if I don't go Division I have failed. FALSE! With the growing number of lacrosse teams across the country, it is true that some division II and III colleges can be a better fit than some Division I schools for certain players.

Strength training is as important when training for lacrosse, as working on the skill components. It is a must that all athletes work out in the gym – a MUST! The thought of lifting weights and working out should not intimidate you; in fact, it should motivate you because it will be helping giving you an edge against your opponents.

Strength training will help you build a strong foundation that allows your body to do more than you could have imagined.

Strength training, and more specifically, weight-lifting and other resistance exercises, helps your ligaments and tendons become stronger. Sprinting is a skill that is improved by strength training because it gives you the ability to strike the ground with a lot more force.

Remember, just because you are strength training, doesn't mean you can ignore your stick skills. You will always need to practice your stick skills no matter how good you get. When you practice your stick skills, please remember that you are practicing to develop habits so that you are able to perform them during the game without thinking about it. For this reason, all stick work, should mirror a game situation as much as possible. Standing 5 feet from the goal and firing shots straight at the middle of the net while standing still is doing nothing to improve your skill level.

The amount of time you spend practicing will vary, depending on the seasons – more to come about seasons later on in the book. It is a good idea to work hard enough to improve your skills by at least five percent each year, or higher.

SKPC CLIENT SHOWCASES

"With the SKPC Med Ball Program Ryan has increased his right and left hand shot speed by 5mph by generating more force...."

We are so happy your program was recommended to us. Ryan has not only improved his skills but we both see that every day he does gain more confidence which was the biggest battle my husband and I always felt needed to change. We always saw his potential at a much higher level than he did. He loves going to lacrosse skills training, never giving us an excuse or reason to try and miss a session and he is actually happier when he comes home even though he may be super exhausted.

The SKPC lacrosse skills training program is ahead of all other lacrosse training programs because it is the total package. The physical aspects of the game are worked on along with the mental attitude that needs to come along with improvement and growth of the individual as a player and young adult. We see a positive change in Ryan and are so thankful we came to Sean Kelly Performance Center.

We will and have recommend SKPC to parents in the Lacrosse community, we cannot say enough about the positives it could do for their child like it did for ours.

Thank you again Sean team!!!!

Tom Leonard, Father of Ryan

CHAPTER TWO: GOAL SETTING

Setting goals as a lacrosse player is very important, which is why we sit down with every athlete that enters our program for at least 45 minutes to discuss the goals that they have. A goal is simply a fantasy unless you, write it down, and commit to achieving it. These goals not only need to be set for each year that you play on a team in school, but goal setting is a process that should take that you can apply to all areas of your life.

Goal setting is not just something that we do to pass time; it is a process that can help you succeed as a lacrosse player.

Some studies have shown that lacrosse players who set goals have the ability to improve their performance anywhere from eight to 16 percent, simply by setting goals.

When you set these goals, you are not only improving your confidence levels, but you are increasing your enthusiasm for the sport.

When you write down your goals, it is important to identify how close you are to achieving them, what is standing in your way, how you plan to remove any barriers, and determine how you will know when you have achieved your goals.

When setting goals, we use the following acronym to guide us through the process **S.M.A.R.T.**:

- **Specific** – Be as specific as possible when setting goals. For example, I will take 50 shots righty and 100 shots lefty 4 days per week is a lot more specific than I will practice my stick skill.

- **Measurement** –We need to quantify our objectives so that we can measure our achievement against them. A measurable goal will usually answer questions such as: How much? How Many? How will I know when it is accomplished?

- **Attainable** – Is this goal something that you will be able to achieve? Don't rely on any extraordinary luck having to happen in order for you to reach your goal. Your goals should stretch you and push you to go further than you ever thought you could, but you don't want them to debilitate you because you know in your heart of hearts that it is not possible.

- **Relevant** – Are the goals you set in alignment with what is truly most important to you?

- **Time-Bound** – A time-bound goal will answer the questions, When will I accomplish this by? Deadlines create a challenge and you will either respond to the challenge or you won't.

At Sean Kelly's Performance Center, we have created a few programs to help our lacrosse players obtain some of the more common goals we see from each of them. One of our programs includes teaching the skills that are required of lacrosse players. General strength, and core strength in particular, is one of the main issues holding players back from improving their skills. To solve this problem, we use a medicine ball in place of a lacrosse stick to drill the motor patterns and muscle memory that a lacrosse player needs to pass and shoot at a high level. On average, every lacrosse athlete in our gym will throw 60 to 80 medicine balls in each session. So the goal has already been set for you, it is something that can be obtained, and with the practice, it will improve your skills. The results that we have seen with this program are awesome. We have seen as much as a 12 miles per hour increase in shot speed over a three-month time period.

SKPC CLIENT SHOWCASES

"In 3 short months David has increased his right hand shot speed by 3mph on his right hand and 2mph on his left handed shot...."

We knew from the start that your program was very different simply by reading through the introductory questionnaire with David. It helped us to formulate his goals and determine what he wanted to get out of the program. Even though he played at a high level of club lacrosse, many of the things that you've taught him he had never been exposed to. Your focus on intan-

gibles, mental preparation, and attention to detail will transform him from a good to a great player and we're looking forward to seeing the results.

He is beginning to understand that preparation starts with dedication months before the season begins, and that he can no longer rely on his physical talent if he wants to excel. His confidence has improved, and your training coupled with our emphasis on making good choices will help him in life, not just on the lacrosse field.

I would highly recommend your program to any athlete looking to take their game to the next level. Your ability to teach and communicate the fundamentals makes the difference between being a good player and a great player. To get to the next level, you cannot depend solely on physical attributes because everyone has that. The difference is mental preparation; focus on fundamentals, and achieving a competitive edge that sets you apart from the other players.

Bill Bavagnoli, Father of David

CHAPTER THREE: MENTAL TOUGHNESS

One of our main responsibilities at Sean Kelly's Performance Center is to help each of our athletes develop great mental toughness so that theycan compete at the highest level of their sport as well as use that same mental toughness to succeed outside of athletics.

We define mental toughness as the ability to perform at your best when your best is needed. It is consistency over time. Anyone can perform great once in a while, being able to consistently perform at your best is what separates the best from the rest.

Remember how we said that most coaches and teams in the lacrosse sporting industry will practice 20 percent of the time, and play the game 80 percent of the time? Well, mental toughness is developed in practice and in the weight room. How can you be expected to perform at your best when your best is needed if you only spend 20% of your time practicing? Focus! It is simply said, but it is not simply done. When training for lacrosse, we always want our athletes to remain focused. There will always be many external distractions that are out of your control as a player. We work with our athletes on focusing on the process and not the outcome. Instead of worrying if you are going to hit the shot, let's focus on the process of shooting and tune everything else out. Hands back, hips toward the target, screw my foot into the ground, and throw my back hip at the target.

Visualization is extremely important when playing the game of lacrosse. The variables of this sport change all of the time, which is why you will need to visualize yourself performing at a high level in situations that you have already seen and ones that you have yet to see.

Some suggestions we give our players when it comes to visualization is to visualize yourself being in the right position at the right time, and flawlessly performing the skills that are expected of you. The more automatic these decisions are, the faster you can play the game and as a result, the more successful you and your team will be. Lacrosse is a fast, physical, unrelenting game and you are going to make mistakes regardless of how much practice and commitment you put into the sport. A mentally tough lacrosse player is able to focus on where the process went wrong and then immediately move on to the next play.

Always stay focused on the process and don't be afraid to make mistakes, have fun. If you follow that formula, you too will be able to perform at your very best, when your very best is needed!

SKPC CLIENT SHOWCASES

"Dom has increased his shot speed by 11mph and has become faster and more explosive improving his 10 yard sprint from 1.9 seconds to 1.66 seconds. He has added 9 inches to his broad jump (6'8" to 7'7") and has more than doubled his push-up and chin-up total, going from 18 to 46 and 5 to 14 respectively..."

"Dedication and Desire" our son had been to several personal trainers and could never make the connection or have that *"ah ha"* moment until SKPC. It was always a struggle to

get him motivated to just attend other gyms or work out centers. Now, thanks to Coach Kelly, our son refuses to miss any work out sessions. Coach Kelly and his staff have made us feel that they have a personal interest in his success and have instilled in him a sense of dedication and the desire to achieve and excel. He now has the tools to be successful on or off the field with a new sense of accomplishment through hard work and perseverance. Thank you SKPC for helping us shape our sons character!

Dominic Branda, Father of Dom

CHAPTER FOUR: TRAINING – SEASONS

If you want to have a healthy career as a student athlete it is crucial that you understand that training is a year round commitment. It is also very important to learn the different phases or seasons of a 12 month training cycle. When practicing for lacrosse, the skill component should be practiced year-round. It is also imperative that you are concentrating on building muscle and gaining weight all-of-the-time. The conditioning component will vary in frequency and intensity throughout the year, and weight training may vary in terms of repetitions and volume.

There are three seasons that a lacrosse player needs to focus on:

Pre-season.

With preseason training, we start with the aerobic aspect, getting you ready for the season. Lacrosse is considered the fastest sport on two feet, meaning training should be a priority. Pre-season goals should be set before the actual training begins. Once training ends, check back to see if you have achieved those goals; if not, add them to your training for the next season or in your spare time.

Some pre-season goals that you may have include:

- Injury Reduction – Learning methods to prevent injury, including mental toughness.

- Individual nutritional plans. Base this plans on your dietary goals.
- Core strengthening.
- Flexibility (and mobility) enhancement.
- Speed, agility, power, and strength training.
- Increase and improve neuromuscular coordination.
- Injury rehabilitation.

In-Season

During our in-season training, probably once or twice a week, we will focus mostly on recovery, mobility, and maintaining and increasing our strength and power.

If you have scheduling conflicts, do everything that you can to make your in-season training a priority. In-season training is necessary because we will focus on keeping you on the field and improving your strength and power so that you are at your best at the start of the post-season when it matters most.

Off-Season

Once the season has ended, you should get ready to begin your off-season nutrition and strength program. The first portion of the off-season program will focus on helping the athlete recover from the season that just concluded.

In the off-season, you do not have as much interaction with your coaches, which is why a lot of responsibility will fall upon the parents and the athletes. You will need to push your children in the right direction, ensuring that they stay on track!

SKPC CLIENT SHOWCASES

"Tyler has dramatically improved his lateral speed decreasing his pro agility time by .4 of a second and his acceleration improving his 10 yard sprint time by .3 seconds. This was made possible by his dedication to improving strength supported by his improvement in both pushups, 10 to 29, and chin ups from 5 to over 15 repetitions..."

Sean and his coaches have worked with my son over the last few months and during that time has made a dramatic impact on Tyler, both physically and mentally. Sean and the SKPC coaches are great motivators; their positive en-

*ergy has clearly transferred over to my son. SK-PC's goal setting was something that I feel was a game changer; Tyler became more driven and was motivated to push himself every day. Sean's training has improved my son's strength, athletic positioning and most importantly, confidence on and off the field. I highly recommend SKPC and **all** that he has to offer.*

Tracy Reed, Mother of Tyler

CHAPTER FIVE: NUTRITION

If you want to perform at the highest level that you are capable of performing at, then you will need to maintain proper nutrition. How your body performs is a direct result of the fuel that you are giving it. It is up to you to make sure you are eating what you are supposed when you are supposed to.

A skilled coach, such as those at Sean Kelly's Performance Center, will provide you with the nutritional advice and guidelines that not only help you remain healthy, but will also help maximize your potential as a player.

Failing to eat breakfast, lunch, and dinner could not only cause athletes to lose a game or play horribly, but these types of bad habits could lead to an injury. It is important that along with the proper meal and diet, you receive adequate fluids to refrain from becoming dehydrated, especially in the warmer months. You should eat:

- Healthy Fats
- Lean Protein
- Quality Carbohydrates

The most important meal of the day is breakfast. This applies to both pre and post workouts. When you are eating after the latter, we suggest that you drink a whey protein shake or even chocolate milk. If your child is in school, they will need to pack their meals to ensure that they eat what they need, and on-time. Breakfast, lunch, and dinner are all important meals, and you should never skip one when you are training for lacrosse.

Snacks are also extremely important when you are training for lacrosse. Protein shakes, hard-boiled eggs, turkey meatballs, Greek yogurt, mixed nuts, and foods in this nature are what your child should eat when training for lacrosse. Hydration is very important, which is why it is being brought up again. We recommend that our enrollees consume around 80 to 100 ounces of water per day. You should limit fluids that do not promote hydration, such as caffeine and beverages with high sugar content.

Always eat and drink healthy to receive the nutrition that you will need!

SKPC CLIENT SHOWCASES

"Rich has added 8mph to his shot speed and has become more confident on and off the field..."

Kelly's Performance Center isn't like a typical gym or all the overpriced clinics I've signed my kids up for over the last twenty years. My son has individual attention from the trainers that has exceeded our expectations. The results are amazing.

The training program consistently and professionally develops a variety of areas that have improved my son as an athlete both physi-

cally and mentally. Perfect technique is expected and encouraged with positive reinforcement that has been highly motivating.

The program has an educational aspect for their athlete that creates awareness for lifelong healthy habits including nutritional plans and goal setting. Coach Kelly and his coaches are teaching my son to be better than yesterday, developing his stick skills, strength, speed, and growing his confidence. These are lifelong skills, not just meant to impact a player's performance on the field, but to create injury free, mentally strong, healthy, goal setting young individuals.

Nicole Thorpe, Mother of Rich

CHAPTER SIX: LACROSSE DRILLS

The lacrosse drills that you learn from the Sean Kelly's Performance Center were designed to help not only our athletes, but coaches as well. You learn the fundamental lacrosse skills necessary to take your game to the next level, as well as the unique skills that will be required of you once you begin playing or coaching lacrosse. Again, it comes down to great coaching, and a lot of repetition.

Some of the drills that you learn

through our lacrosse training program include:

- Catching and Passing Drill Progressions (wall ball and partner passing progressions from stationary to on the run)

- Defensive Drill Progressions (footwork, stance, body position, ground balls, and stick checking progressions)

- Dodging Drill Progressions (learn to execute individual moves required for midfielders and attackman)

- Goalie Drill Progressions (Footwork, stance, body and stick positioning, communication, and clearing

- Speed Drill Progressions (Learn proper linear and lateral running techniques as well as proper acceleration and deceleration)

- Shooting Drill Progressions (from stationary to on the run shooting)

- Ground Ball Drill Progressions (proper form and body position as well as what to do after you scoop the ball)

- and more…

We will show each of our athletes each concept, in a variety of ways to keep the atmosphere new and exciting. We have put together a part-whole system of teaching each skill. We break each skill down into small pieces so that our athletes have a much better chance of being able to digest so much information.

They will continue to repeat these skills until they can perform them at a fast pace with a minimal amount of mistakes. They will then be able to take the skills they have learned and transfer them into on the field results.

CHAPTER SEVEN: WRONG DIRECTION

Going in the wrong direction is something that many people do, which is why this lacrosse program is important. So many individuals view lacrosse as a club sport; this is the wrong assumption to make. There's more to this sport than running up and down a field; it takes hard work, dedication, and lots of training.

Many students are under the assumption that they do not need to lift, run, or maintain a healthy diet, amongst other things. This is why so many players do not progress after "training" for the sport; they don't think training is actually involved. Running out on the field without studying the sport or receiving proper training can lead to various issues, including injury. Just like any other sport, if you want to succeed, you have to work hard. You couldn't go on the basketball court and immediately guard a player who has been training for years; if you did, you would surely make countless mistakes, and you would put yourself – and others - at the risk of injury. This is true with lacrosse.

This thinking is what's wrong with so many youth across the country, and it is why parents should enroll them in a training program. The more they know; the more they can progress.

This training program will help develop a player, and determine what their weaknesses are, including mental weakness. Parents should never let their children play lacrosse, or any other sport, without being trained properly. Preparation is everything, and this training program was designed to prepare players in school, as well as those well into their careers.

Would you take a test without preparing? Would you give a speech without preparing the speech? Would you present to a client without prepping first? No! Therefore, you need to prepare for lacrosse by signing up for the training program offered at the Sean Kelly Performance Center. Do not make the wrong assumptions, or take the wrong direction... There are no short-cuts in life, or lacrosse.

TAKE THE NEXT STEP...

We train our lacrosse players in every aspect of the sport, which is something that you cannot find elsewhere. To take your level of skills and knowledge to the next level, it is imperative that you focus on all areas of the sport, because if you don't, somebody else will. You will find exactly what you need to master the mental and physical aspects of lacrosse; you just need to show the willingness and commitment necessary to learn all that we teach at Sean Kelly's Performance Center.

Practice makes habits, and great practice will help you form great habits. Sign-up for our lacrosse training program and see your results surpass your loftiest goals.

Sean has a truly unique work ethic, along with the ability to apply special attention to detail. When it pertains to training lacrosse players, these two characteristics are extremely important. Sean has experience as both a player and as someone on the educational side of this sport itself. Regardless of which side you are on, the importance of hard work and dedication is a necessity, pertaining to the Lacrosse sport.

The crucial and knowledge and experience that players need to progress within this field can be learned through this lacrosse program. Each athlete will receive attention-to-detail instruction that they need, ensuring that each specific athlete is satisfied.

If you want to progress in your athletic career, or as a student lacrosse player, this is the perfect program for you!

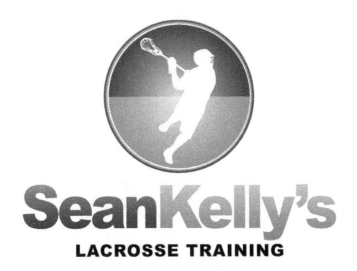

LACROSSE TRAINING